The
ART *of*
HUMANE
EDUCATION

Donald Phillip Verene

Cornell
University
Press

*Ithaca
and
London*

First published 2002 by Cornell University Press

Printed in the United States of America

Library of Congress Cataloging-in-Publication Data

Verene, Donald Phillip, 1937–
   The art of humane education / Donald Phillip Verene.
      p. cm.
Includes bibliographical references and index.
   ISBN 0-8014-4039-4 (cloth : alk. paper)
   1. Education, Humanistic.   2. Education—Philosophy.   3. Teaching.   I.
Title.
   LC1011 .V45 2002
   370.11'2—dc21   2002002085

Cornell University Press strives to use environmentally
responsible suppliers and materials to the fullest extent
possible in the publishing of its books. Such materials
include vegetable-based, low-VOC inks and acid-free papers
that are recycled, totally chlorine-free, or partly composed
of nonwood fibers. For further information, visit our website
at www.cornellpress.cornell.edu.

Cloth printing   10   9   8   7   6   5   4   3   2   1

For this knowledge is not something that can be put into words like other sciences; but after long-continued intercourse between teacher and pupil, in joint pursuit of the subject, suddenly, like light flashing forth when a fire is kindled, it is born in the soul and straightway nourishes itself.

—PLATO, *Seventh Letter*

Contents

Preface

G. W. F. Hegel says that a preface
stands outside the work and purports to give the reader a
statement of the subject without the reader having entered into it. A preface misleads us from the beginning to
think that an external grasp of the subject is possible, but
the matters the work treats can be known only on their
own terms. To discuss human education is always to be
in the position of Hegel's preface. One can acquire an education by becoming a student, but an education cannot
be acquired by a discussion of what education is. Yet an
education is an ultimate possession of an individual, and
we cannot refrain from speaking about it for whatever
good this might achieve.

In like manner, there is no way to teach what teaching

is through a discussion of the nature of teaching. Perhaps the most useful things to say about teaching reduce to tips on what to do in the classroom, the formulation of syllabuses and examinations, and the conception of assignments and evaluation of papers. The smallest alteration in format can often achieve a great change in a pedagogical situation. But there remain philosophical issues of pedagogy: what it is as a whole and the truth of its ideals.

My aim is to present in brief a view of pedagogy in both a theoretical sense and a practical sense. By pedagogy I mean the study of the principles of formal education that are the basis of the art of teaching. My approach is grounded in my own field of philosophy. What I say may be regarded as part of the "tradition of the new" in that what is new is really a revival of the most old. I regard philosophy as one of the humanities, and because of this I believe what I say may be applicable to the humanities in general. I would define the humanities as philosophy, history, and the languages and literatures, in other words, those fields that study arts, letters, and morals. The humanities offer education in what was once called the Republic of Letters. A humane education includes the study of both the sciences and the humanities. Although my emphasis is on humanistic education, from time to time I have attempted to state what seem to me parallel points for scientific education.

Humane letters have been criticized since René Descartes excluded them from his method of right reasoning in *Discourse on Method* (1637). Descartes is the father of modernity, and he founded his method of reasoning on the exclusion of the arts of memory, poetry, rhetoric, and narrative from the search for truth. These are the forms of thought crucial to civil wisdom and self-knowledge that were the products of the ancients and the Renaissance humanists. Despite Descartes, the study of humane letters has remained, but it is always in danger of passing out of the curriculum. It remains a beggar who will not quite leave the premises.

The views that follow are in the form of letters, the letter being the precursor of the essay. Thus I have thought of Michel de Montaigne's *Essays*, which he addresses both to himself and to the world, and of Friedrich Schiller's letters *On the Aesthetic Education of Man*. I have also thought of Horace's letter to the Piso family, in which he states his *Art of Poetry*. My letters are not real letters but are devices to engage the reader. The correspondents are not personalities but personae that convey common thoughts. The letter, the oration, and the essay are the common forms of the humanist. In these forms of expression the self attempts to speak about itself. The primary concern of the human self is its own education. The primary concern of the professional humanist who is a teacher is to speak to this aim and to promote its satisfaction.

Much of what follows will go against the current. I do not expect the reader to agree. My wish is that these thoughts may be a pleasure to read and that they may be suggestive. They may recall for the reader views of humane education that are lost or all but lost in the modern curriculum and in the modern notion of teaching as based in consumer satisfaction. The modern student is a consumer of a product made by the teacher. At the end of the course, the student completes the course questionnaire, which is nearly the same as those cards found in motel rooms or on restaurant tables, asking the customer to evaluate the accommodations, the food, the service.

The teacher is a member of the service industry who needs to show the administration that the product is working. The teacher, caught in the middle, needs feedback; the lot of the modern teacher is constant improvement and adjustment of the classroom experience in the hope of being evaluated well. As a functional system, each factor adjusts itself to the other through a process of administrative and student-consumer oversight and vigilant self-improvement of the service of the teacher. It is a system that never sleeps. Missing is the ancient standard of excellence that can be had only by hierarchy, judgment, and eccentricity. None of these is on the course questionnaire.

Modern teaching is classroom management and career management, an extension of administrative aims to the learning process. Students exit the university having learned the art of taking courses and developing a résumé of their years as a student. What has been learned is not so much chemistry, or history, or philosophy as a corporate sense of life, how to pass a course, how to participate. How to think or how to read, if learned, are fringe benefits, for what has most been learned is how to graduate. It is Friedrich Nietzsche's cheerful scene of the theoretical man. For the humanist who looks on it, it is a source of melancholy. It is my belief that the humanist ideal of self-knowledge can still be transmitted to the few who respond to it when they hear it, and that the many may benefit from it even if they leave without fully accepting its education.

The first two letters speak to how the humanist may approach the process of pedagogy. They address the question of how to teach and the forces of the contemporary university that surround teaching and learning. The second two letters speak to the subject matter of the humanist. They address the question of what to teach and the medium in which this can occur: ideas and books.

The proximate cause of these letters is my sometime seminar on pedagogy for graduate students in philosophy. The ideas herein go back to my own liberal arts education, to my study with the humanist philosopher A. W. Levi, and my conversations, over many years, with the Renaissance humanist scholar Ernesto Grassi, in Switzerland, in Germany, and in Italy at his villa on the island of Ischia near Naples.

I thank my colleagues who so kindly read and offered many useful comments on the manuscript: Thora Bayer, Martine Brownley, James Gouinlock, Ann Hartle, Donald Livingston, Denis Mickiewicz, and Carl Page. I also thank Molly Black Verene for her assistance and enduring attention. I thank Ralph Smith, editor of the *Journal of Aesthetic Education*, in which earlier versions of the first two of these letters appeared (vol. 33, no. 2).

The
ART *of*
HUMANE
EDUCATION

1 ON PEDAGOGICAL ELOQUENCE
(To a Friend)

I RECEIVED your letter asking me to express some views on pedagogy, particularly in relation to language and the nature of instruction. As a scientist engaged in theoretical research and not in teaching, you have not, as you say, been in a classroom in a long time. You are quite right in thinking that much has changed since your own college courses in the liberal arts and sciences. Your concern is with the education of your own children, how they may obtain a sense of wisdom and virtue such as the ancients and the humanists at one time professed, in addition to an education in the sciences.

I willingly undertake to respond to your request, but as you know, I have never claimed to have a knowledge of the subject of pedagogy, if indeed it can be called a subject at all. I wish to divide your request in two. Here I wish to address the question of language, and in another letter I will confront the claims of instruction. What I say here concerns pedagogical eloquence, in other words, the rhetorical basis of the art of human education.

Such eloquence is not separate from eloquence in general, but in our time eloquence has disappeared from the classroom, as it has more widely disappeared from modern thought and life. In his last public statement, his address to the Academy of Oziosi, Giambattista Vico said: "I hold the opinion that if eloquence does not regain the luster of the Latins and Greeks in our time, when our sciences have made progress equal to and perhaps even greater than theirs, it will be because the sciences are taught completely stripped of every badge of eloquence."

In the humanist tradition that runs from the ancients through the Renaissance, the badge of eloquence has always been worn by wisdom. The ideal that the teacher shares with the poet and the orator has been "wisdom that speaks." The purpose of the poet and the speaker since Cicero and Horace has been to delight, instruct, and move. This has been the aim of the teacher, especially the teacher of humane letters, of which philosophy at its best is a part. As the love of wisdom, philosophy is also the love of the language that can impart wisdom. How would wisdom speak, if not eloquently?

As Quintilian says, *eloqui* is to run through all there is on a subject, all that the speaker has conceived. Eloquence refers not to fine phraseology but to the speech that captures the whole of a subject. This can include digressions. Demosthenes with his "invincible enthymeme" was said to take his audience far afield from his subject and then make a connection that brought his point crashing down upon his audience like a flash of lightning. The digression within the whole, in which it is said all true philosophy is done, is a characteristic of copious speech. *Copia* is speaking variously at once so that all aspects of a subject are touched upon. Today, in an age missing rhetoric, eloquence is equated with elegance of expression. Elegance is how a particular thing is said, often in a way so as to strike the memory—a turn of phrase. Eloquence is to speak on the whole of the subject and is thus wisdom speaking. Wisdom as understood by the ancients and as reported by Cicero is "a knowledge of things divine and human."

Knowledge is associated with a speech of the part, much like Descartes would desire in his method. Wisdom is dialectical speech that combines and moves in terms of opposites, the ultimate opposites being the divine and human. Dialectical speech on a subject activates the minds of the audience and causes movement. The speech of the part is fixed, often propositional, descriptive, and argumentative. It focuses the mind's eye to see as if by lamplight in the dark. Eloquent speech proceeds as if by sunlight, even if its seeing is incomplete.

Eloquence, the speech of the whole, like poetic speech must delight, instruct, and move. It must delight in the sense that it is more important that a proposition be interesting than that it be true. Truth, of course, adds interest. The speech of the teacher must attract interest in order to say the true things that instruct. Finally, it must move. It must affect the passions and thus change the person in some way so that the truth of the instruction is taken up in the self. If this is not accomplished then no education has occurred. Education depends upon the metamorphosis of the self toward wisdom. At least, this is the character of humane education, if not all education. The purpose of teaching is to produce a self that can think. Information and skills will fall into line behind this. I share your view that too much emphasis is placed today on information, which in itself is not thought.

The power to move is associated with what Longinus calls the sublime. Sublimity is the power of the word to transport the audience to a new level. This can emerge from the whole tissue of the composition, the way its facts and truths are woven together, or it can occur in a flash. As described by Longinus, this momentary sense of sublimity is very like the sense of epiphany that so interested James Joyce. Longinus says, "A well-timed flash of sublimity scatters everything before it like a bolt of lightning and reveals the full power of the speaker at a single stroke" (1.4). This momentary sense of sublimity is an ideal toward which any teacher strives. The sublimity of the composition as a whole may be more accessible since it can be worked at. It is likely that the momentary sense of sublimity presupposes the sublimity of the whole in order to have a context in which to occur.

Longinus determines five sources of sublimity. The teacher might strive for these in every verbal composition: the command of solid or full-blooded ideas; the inspiration of emotion; the proper use of figures of thought and speech (such as metaphor, metonymy, synecdoche, irony, as well as syllogisms, inductions, and analogies); above these, nobility of phrase (choice of words, diction); and general effect of dignity and elaboration. Especially important to this last source but crucial to all is "synthesis," the arrangement of words into a whole (8.1–2). Longinus speaks of this sense of synthesis as being like a melody, which is not only a natural instrument of pleasure but an instrument of grandeur and emotion. He holds that a sublime composition is a kind of "melody in words"; these words must be part of human nature and reach not only the ears but the soul (39.3). Such a melody of words stirs a myriad of moods, thoughts, and memories.

You will agree, I think, that it is important to teach the subject as a whole. Eloquent speech presents the whole of a subject, and when it is sublime it is musical. This melodiousness or synthesis depends on proportion and might be considered architectural. It keeps all parts of the subject in their proper proportion to each other and by implication communicates a sense of the whole subject being treated. The best examples are to be found in Cicero's orations or in Pico della Mirandola's oration on human dignity or in Vico's oration on heroic education. Anyone who teaches or wishes to teach may find such an ideal out of reach. But why settle for less? Is the ideal not true, is it incorrect, or in some way less than what should be aimed at?

We live in an age that is typified by what the French thinker Jacques Ellul has called "the humiliation of the word." Against this modern form of humiliation I have placed the ancient humanists, who believed in the word and its essential connection to truth, not just truth as a metaphor for certain conventions, political interests, or historical context, but truth as the True which is the whole. The classroom is the one place where the word might survive. The word has been replaced by the image in politics, by technique in the sciences and everyday life, and by hermeneutics in the literary and critical arts.

The humiliation of the word has already entered the classroom. But there, in the mouth of the teacher, its humiliation might confront the sublimity of speech practiced as an art that extends the natural disposition of the teacher to speak and to speak well. It is the task of the teacher to learn the nearly lost art of eloquence of which the ancients speak. The teacher may need to learn this alone or, if fortunate, by mimetic absorption of a model, if one can be found.

At this point you might ask whether there are any starting points that may be useful to eloquent teaching and the teaching of eloquence. This is a difficult subject, but certain things can be said. The principles of rhetorical composition provide a guide for directing students in reading a text. Vico endorses a doctrine of reading a text three times: first for the sense of the work as a whole, second for grasping the transitions of thought, and third for attention to the turns of phrase. This sequence reflects the first three of Quintilian's principles of composition. Composition requires *inventio* or the gathering of materials, *dispositio* or their arrangement, and *elocutio* or their formulation in language. The threefold method of reading follows the composition of the text itself, the phases the author has necessarily passed through, whether consciously or unconsciously, in the production of the work.

When the reader passes through these analogous phases, he or she makes the work again, now as the reader's own product. The work's truth is made in the reader's own mind. What the author has once made is made again by the reader. Students will certainly master any assignment by enacting this doctrine. It can be recommended to them as a method of study. In such a program of reading it is good to read one text against another, in a dialectical fashion. Vico did this by reading the moderns against the ancients on successive days. Thus he read Cicero side by side with Boccaccio, Virgil with Dante, and Horace with Petrarch. But one might read Descartes side by side with Sigmund Freud, Edward Gibbon with Oswald Spengler, Henry James with James Joyce, or works of contemporary thought might be tested against works of traditional thought. This method is limited only by the combinations one might consider.

In composing lectures the teacher will naturally follow Quintilian's principles of composition, for lecture materials must be amassed, arranged, and expressed in language. There are two further steps associated with the presentation of what is composed—*memoria* or recalling what is to be said, and *pronuntiatio*, the speaking out of what is to be said. These steps are classically associated with the law courts but are applicable to the oration or the lecture. The author of the *Ad herennium* says: "Now let me turn to the treasure-house of the ideas supplied by Invention, to the guardian of all the parts of rhetoric, the Memory" (3.16.28).

The eloquent teacher can strive to speak without notes. This requires an "inner writing," a means whereby topics to be spoken about can be committed to memory in advance. Aristotle says: "But one must get hold of a starting point. This explains why it is that persons are supposed to recollect sometimes by starting from 'places.' " He concludes: "It seems in general that the middle point among all things is a good starting point" (*Rh.* 452a14–19). The middle point is a commonplace from which the speaker can draw forth what is to be said. The commonplace (*topos*) may be an image or a general idea that the teacher and the students hold in common. Shaftesbury speaks of *sensus communis* not as a form of pretheoretical thinking but as communal sense, the sense of things held in common by a society. This is common sense formed by human beings making sense to-gether through their passions, language, customs, and laws. The excellence of the teacher's starting points for any composition depends upon the ability to locate and employ these commonplaces to strike the right chords.

Memory has a natural affinity for physical place. An inner writing can be created by associating in advance each of the solid and full-blooded ideas the teacher wishes to express with a physical place, a particular room, or an object within a room or space. Then, thinking of this place brings to mind the idea, formed through a topos that makes it initially familiar to the hearers. This method goes back to Simonides of Ceos, who is said to have identified the dead crushed in the collapse of a banquet hall by recalling, for their grieving relatives, the place at which each was seated.

All teaching depends upon memory in all of its powers. It is no accident that Hesiod calls Memory (Mnemosyne) the Mother of the Muses, who are themselves the arts of humanity. As with the poet, the Muse is always needed for the teacher to speak, and especially needed to produce the moment of sublimity of which Longinus speaks. The teacher must believe in the Muse. To believe simply in a logical order of ideas would be to produce dull or cynical speech. I know from our contact over the years that you hold that science cannot be satisfied with mere logical order and evidence but requires inspiration and insight to do its work.

As Hesiod explains, the Muses sing of what was, is, and is to come. It is generally true of eloquent speech that in its wholeness on a subject it brings the past together with the present and the future. The teacher, through eloquence, can master time in this way. The classroom can be a precinct in which the arts of humanity and the achievements of the sciences are displayed—a museum, a term that derives from the Muses. Plato's Academy contained a museum. In the classroom, although usually a spare and unadorned space today, the teacher can attempt connection with the Muses and their Mother. There is no Muse assigned to teaching or learning, although Clio, who governs narrative, and Urania, who governs the heavens (nature), must be important. The teacher must try to reach the Muses' own source of instruction, Memory. The Muses may inspire and create the classroom as a momentary museum, but Memory is the ultimate guide for the arts of teaching and learning. Her powers are at the heart of the process.

The *pronuntiatio* of the teacher, the oral elegance of language, requires the prior reading of great works and absorption of the third phase of the doctrine of reading—the turn of phrase. Reading great works at least must set the standard if it is not actually the practical guide. The teacher cannot produce proper language from a vacuum. It will depend upon the teacher's own *paideia*. It is widely known that the teacher should say everything three times in order that the students not only hear it but become conscious of it. In terms of the principles of eloquence, this means that the teacher should say what the idea is as a whole, then show its implications, and finally find a turn of phrase that can capture it and impress it in the student's memory.

In teaching the *Phaedo*, the teacher might first focus on the sense in which it is an extension of Socrates' speech in the *Apology*, further showing his friends what true philosophy is. Then the teacher could give attention to the parts of the dialogue and to the steps in the arguments for immortality. Finally, the teacher might focus on the famous expression that "those who rightly philosophize are practicing to die" (*hoi orthos philosophountes apothneskein meletosi*). Each part of this threefold expression might be separated from the others by digressions to achieve a dialectic of speech and a constant recall. But the mind is always fixed three times on the meaning of each solid, full-blooded idea.

A word may be said about the relation of eloquence and argument. In the *Phaedo* Socrates warns against becoming a misologist because argument can never settle anything. Despite this defect of argument—that for every argument there is always a good counterargument—we should not become enemies of argument. In intellectual exchange argument can serve to bring out the features of a claim. But in our time argument, especially in philosophy, has become an intellectual fetish. We encounter those who proceed as though thought itself were argument. There are those who think philosophy in particular is about the construction of arguments. It is an easy idea.

What is meant by argument can vary from the Latin sense of *argumentum*, the theme of a speech, to argument as a proof having the form of a deduction. But if everything is an argument, nothing is an argument. And if arguments must be proofs in order to be arguments, there will be too few of them to be useful. Argument is natural to philosophers and students of philosophy, and there is little need to teach it. There are those who would just look for arguments in a text, thus missing the text itself—the whole of what the philosopher wrote. Argument is always a partial way of thinking and presupposes a whole speech in which it makes sense, whether this whole is explicit or assumed.

Arguments may be elegant, but they are never eloquent,

for arguments are never in themselves wisdom. Instruction that regards the use of language to create arguments as the high point of the interchange between teacher and student is mistaken. It trivializes education. In place of argument as the leading form of instruction I would put the question as the fundamental device of philosophical inquiry. But I shall say more on this in another letter. As you have said to me on several occasions, argument has its use in science, but in science evidence and experiment can do what argument alone can never do.

Concerning eloquence and writing I can say no more than what Vico has said in glossing Horace. Writing presumes a tutorial relationship between teacher and student. Vico says Horace has condensed in three lines all the art required to use language well in prose and in verse. " 'Right thinking is the first principle and source of writing,' because there is no eloquence without truth and dignity; of these two parts wisdom is composed. 'Socratic writings [probably meaning the writings of Plato, Xenophon, and Aeschines] will direct you in the choice of subjects,' that is, the study of morals, which principally informs the wisdom of man, to which more than in the other parts of philosophy Socrates divinely applied himself, whence of him it was said: 'Socrates recalled moral philosophy from the heavens.' And 'when the subject is well conceived, words will follow spontaneously,' because of the natural bond by which we claim language and heart to be held fast together, for to every idea its proper voice stands naturally attached. Thus, eloquence is none other than wisdom speaking."

Here we find analogies to Quintilian's principles of composition. Moral philosophy will direct *inventio*, right thinking will provide for *dispositio*, and the proper voice for every idea will accomplish *elocutio*. Writing is thus to be taught as a formation of the soul and not as a simple exercise in communication or information. In such a precept the word can never be humiliated on the page. Is this too much? Is it a false ideal? If so, then what ideal should be held up to the student who wishes to enter in some measure the Republic of Letters? What else is the student to be taught except the arts of thinking, writing, and speaking in their fullest dimension? This would seem enough and also more than is ever possible. Or should a pragmatism rule, that has no concern with excellence? I think not.

Finally, the classroom is the crucible of eloquence as it guides pedagogy. It is the anatomical theater in which the subject matter is to be cut at its joints and displayed to the mind's eye. It is a crucible because in it the idea, or the narration of ideas, becomes truly finite. It must find its form for both the teacher and the student in a very limited time; most often today it is the fifty-minute hour. I shall remark on the nature of discussion in my subsequent letter, should you still have patience for it. Here I describe the possibilities of the lecture session.

Of course the teacher should lecture. How else can pedagogical eloquence be realized? How else can the student, wishing to know what it means to think, witness live, self-directed thinking—"wisdom speaking"? In approaching the lecture, which may be interrupted by questions, consider the time. For the first five minutes the students are coming to order, and attendance may be taken. Then the teacher begins, and has only a good twenty minutes to develop an idea, to say it three times, to digress, give examples, and display irony. As the end of the first half-hour approaches the teacher should take several minutes to be irrelevant, to set the stage for a second idea, to establish a new beginning. The lecturer then has twenty minutes to develop this second idea. At the very end the students are restless. In the last minutes the instructor takes the opportunity to assert simple authority, to call attention to the next assignment, to the coming examination, paper, or other requirement. Then it is over. What the students take away is the completeness or the incompleteness of the occasion, what has been eloquently impressed on the memory.

With this I conclude. I hope that this has fulfilled at least some of your request to learn my views on teaching. I assure you that I make no special claim for them. They are only the meditations of one who has attempted to discover some of the principles of the art of human education, which, I believe, was your reason for writing me.

2 ON PEDAGOGICAL AUTHORITY

From your response to my first letter I see that you have taken my remarks kindly and have understood the spirit in which they are formulated. You express some skepticism as to whether teaching is a gift of nature or an art that can be taught. The ancients raised the same question about oratory. I have portrayed teaching as a part of oratory, and I can offer no more of an answer than I have already given. Like oratory, teaching requires a natural gift, but it is also an art that, like all the other humane arts, can be learned only mimetically. Some things can also be said of it in the form of principles derived from the phenomenon itself. As some are born tone-deaf and cannot be musical, there are those who can never teach. But most, if they wish, have some aptitude for it, and this aptitude can be developed into an art.

Immanuel Kant in his third *Critique* says that *ars oratoria* "deserves no respect whatsoever," a sentiment that he shares with the "illustrious Locke," who saw the words of eloquent speech as "perfect cheats." Yet it is said that Kant conducted his courses by concentrating on the expression of the student in the lecture hall who appeared least to understand what he was saying, and, when he saw signs of comprehension in that student, he knew that the others would have already grasped his idea.

Kant's rather stern yet tolerant procedure was not followed by Hegel. Hegel, at least in the lecture rooms of Jena, spoke, it is said, in a kind of *raptus* which invaded the room and took the students up in it, although it was an appeal to their reason, not simply to passion. It is also said that Hegel spoke in a halting manner, but he did nothing without passion and was from his early years schooled in rhetoric. The principles of rhetoric have recently been recognized as consciously present in the arrangement of his *Phenomenology of Spirit*. Hegel claimed not simply the love of wisdom but wisdom itself. His principle that the "True is the whole" is not only the ancient claim of the wholeness of wisdom but the claim made of language by eloquence. The model for pedagogical *mimesis* may lie between the classroom styles of Kant and Hegel.

As promised, I turn to the second of your requests, that concerning the claims of instruction. My remarks on this subject concern the question of pedagogical authority. In our day there is much confusion about the question of authority in general, and this confusion has entered the process of education, where it has received no resolution. Authority can be either imposed or natural to the situation. If it is imposed, it is external to affairs over which it claims control, and it is always in principle rightfully open to challenge, even though its imposition may be fortunate and desirable. If authority is natural to a situation, it arises from within the actual order of the activity and can be easily recognized by all as required for the activity to be what it is. When this is the case authority is truly jurisprudential, and the common example is the law.

Another example of natural authority is pedagogy. The activity of pedagogy involves the subject matter, the teacher, and the student. Only the subject matter and the teacher have authority. The student has no authority but engages in learning the subject with the aim of acquiring authority or some authority in it. Authority resides first in the subject matter, which in humanistic instruction is often in the text to be studied. In the sciences it is often in the experiment to be done and in the theory and the evidence for it to be mastered. Authority lies second in the teacher as one who can profess the subject. The teacher is always answerable to the subject, and in this sense the subject stands above both the teacher and the student. Allegiance to any other reality than the subject is a corruption of the pedagogical process.

The subject to be taught and to be learned always involves purpose. The telos of the subject removes any claim of the politics of the classroom and sets a standard of jurisprudential behavior. Everyone adjusts to what is naturally right and prudent to enable consideration of the subject matter. Direct attention to the subject matter has a civilizing effect. It creates a common aim. Interaction among members of the class is not its purpose. Focus on the subject matter relieves all concern with politics and psychodynamics and allows ordinary manners and character to govern. Thus, to teach the early pages of Thomas Mann's *Death in Venice* is to allow the passages themselves to reign, what is said on the page and what can be made out of it in interpretation. The teacher may bring out the connection between Aschenbach's name and the various senses of *Asche* in German, as in the expression "*Friede seiner Asche!*" ("May his ashes rest in peace!"), or in *Aschenbecher* (ashtray) as a receptacle for what is consumed, exhausted. The teacher may point out the contrast between Aschenbach's status as the great German scholar and the familiar, obsequious way in which he is addressed by the Italian ticket seller, as he buys his passage on a steamer to Venice from Pola. The students may proceed to advance hypotheses of interpretation and to work with the teacher on ways to make the pages come alive and yield up formulations of meaning.

The authority of the teacher is maintained by the ability to keep attention on the subject, which in turn establishes the prudentiality of the proceedings. In this regard the teacher is like the judge whose authority is maintained by comprehension and proper application of the law. The teacher is always in a sense a student, of course, for like the law, the subject is always more than can be mastered. The teacher differs from the student in terms of what the teacher knows. The teacher knows more because the teacher has already followed the path the students will follow. It is the natural relation of the old and the young, crucial to any society.

At this point you might ask how the authority of the subject matter is established. In the sciences it is established by reported research that is immediately and continually progressive, one decade of knowledge surpassed by the next. The sciences work with the most recent, and that is their strength. The canon in the sciences is what has just now been found to be true and what further, on this basis, can be found to be true.

Instruction in humane letters depends upon the authority of a canon. A canon is objective in the sense that it is the result of tradition, that is to say, the result of human memory. A canon is remembered and revived through its comprehension by successive generations. It is the thing to learn, to think about, and ultimately to add to. A canon is usually a series of books running back through history that contains the self-identity of a people. They can identify with it and continually rediscover their identity through it.

The Western canon is a historical series of works going back to Homer, but a canon can also be a set of works that lie equally at the origin, such as the five classics at the beginning of Chinese culture, the *I Ching* or *Book of Changes* being most prominent among them, the others being *Shih* or Odes, *Shu* or History (documents compiled in the sixth century), *Ch'un Ch'iu* (Annals of Confucius), and *Shih-li* (*I-li*) or Rituals. A canon is just tradition in intellectual terms. A canon is no more definite or ill-defined than is the human phenomenon of tradition.

If there is no respect for tradition, that is, no piety toward our own self-identity, our own memory, then the canon is lost, and we become politically motivated agents in a game of exchanges. Plato's claim that knowledge is power is inverted, and power becomes the same as knowledge. Like tradition in human affairs, which works are included in a canon can never be clearly or finally determined. A canon is fundamentally a claim that there *are* great books, but which books are the definitive great books will always be ambiguous. This question determines much of humanistic thought.

Against the idea of a canon is the view that all works are political documents. Those who hold this view cannot think beyond cultural politics to cultural memory. They regard all cultural memory as a product of cultural politics. They feel they have peeped through the keyhole of history and have seen what was really happening. What appeared to be the attempt by the great works to formulate essential truths and self-knowledge were really acts of class, gender, or race interest and are acts of self-deception. The great narratives of truth are lies.

The adherents to this view have drawn Nietzsche's conclusion in his fragment "On Truth and Lie in an Extra-Moral Sense": "What, then, is truth? A mobile army of metaphors, metonyms, and anthropomorphisms—in short, a sum of human relations, which have been enhanced, transposed, and embellished poetically and rhetorically, and which after long use seem firm, canonical, and obligatory to a people: truths are illusions about which one has forgotten that this is what they are; metaphors which are worn out and without sensuous power; coins which have lost their pictures and now matter only as metal, no longer as coins."

Those opposed to a canon face the problem that they have discovered a truth about truth that is not subject to its own conditions. They must face the problem of justifying this new colossal truth derived through the keyhole, or they must claim that this truth, newly discovered, upon which their position is based is itself a political stance. All is reduced to exchanges of power. There is no culture, nothing that transcends individual or group interest.

For the humanist all is an act of memory applied to the present. It is memory that humanizes. In the classroom this means that the classics, as well as works of contemporary importance, are studied. The importance of contemporary works is determined by how they confront the past, how close they seem to come to the excellence of the classics. The teacher needs a good memory for what is said in the texts, and the students need to develop memory as well as ingenuity, or what in Latin is called *ingenium*, the ability to bring two otherwise disparate things together and perceive a relationship.

This ability is required for Longinus's sense of the sublime, especially the epiphany of the momentary sublime.

Ingenium is required for the formation of both metaphor and hypothesis—the required starting points of thought. *Ingenium* is needed in both the humanities and the sciences. I doubt you will disagree with this. Students must not only master the power of memory, they must experience the power of *ingenium* in order to create new postulates of thought. Aristotle says that the greatest thing to be by far is a master of metaphor, for it cannot be learned and it is a sign of genius.

There is an old distinction that there are those who know, those who can come to know when taught by those who know, and those who do not know. A similar distinction can be found in Eastern literature—that there are three disciples of Zen. There are those who know Zen, those who tend the temples and grounds, and then there are the rice bags and coat hangers. The authority of the teacher comes directly from that of the subject matter and conventionally from the community of knowers who recognize others like themselves.

Formal programs of instruction that offer certificates and degrees attempt to emulate this recognition but often fail, perhaps more than half the time. Thus only some with degrees are really knowers with more than programmatic authority. Only some of those with degrees and positions in philosophy are philosophers, only some with degrees in history really have a fundamental, historical sense of things, and only some with degrees in literature are truly literary. There are always more bodies, so to speak, than there are souls.

This discrepancy causes a problem for the student,

who can be counted among those who can come to know if taught by those who know. Degree and teaching position are no indication of mastery of the natural and true authority of subject matter. Education as an institution is a theater of impostors. Only by listening and asking questions can the student attempt to distinguish the teachers from those who appear to be so and who often are so full of techniques as to seem even to themselves to be teachers. There is no art known by which those who wish to come to know can make a selection. It is, so far as I can see, in the hands of the gods, coupled with the natural wit of the student. The best guide may be to compare the teacher and teaching with what the student can find in the canon and other important works.

One sign by which the student may judge is the presence or absence of eloquence. Teachers motivated by eloquence attempt to speak wholly on a subject, since the whole is where its life is. Teachers not motivated by eloquence tend to be either dull or comedic. The dull teacher may have knowledge but no true language for it. Such a teacher can instruct but has no ability to delight or move, and thus is boring. The comedic teacher is shallow and a menace to the subject matter, because such a performer is a sham. The comedic teacher is a sophist and enjoys the success that the sophist often enjoys. The comedic teacher's aim is audience satisfaction and often such teachers are the recipients of awards. Neither boredom nor comedy is sustaining for the student. The truth of the subject matter is what makes possible both the teacher and the student. The dedication to this truth is the basis for the community of scholars, the Republic of Letters, the great conversation, and the conception of the liberal arts itself.

Outside this community, this Republic, this conversation, are those who do not know. They are in a sense the rest of the university, not its ordinary employees, its honest workers, for they might work anywhere, but its administrators and professional hangers-on. The modern university is not a community of scholars but a corporation with a managerial class composed of academics who have left teaching not to return or who received degrees and never taught at all but went directly into administration. These and other professionals make up a class of their own, with their own national organizations, publications, careers, and awards.

The administration of the university is an ever present authority with which the teacher must contend. Its power is political and financial. Its authority is not pedagogical, and its language is not eloquent. The work of the administrator is to direct the work of the community of scholars, to the extent that such survives in the corporate landscape of the modern university. Like Hegel's *Herr*, his master in the master-servant relationship, the administration has no true object of work. Its "work," like that of the master, is to ensure the work of others and to live from it.

The administration's reality depends upon the extent to which it can affect and order the process of teaching and learning. Thus with the help of certain faculty it constantly creates programs to improve teaching, to give awards and grants, and to conduct evaluations. Administration is never content simply to concern itself with the pure business of the university, paying its bills, maintaining its buildings. It sees itself as necessary to the process between teacher and student. But it constantly interrupts that process.

Constant evaluation is an instrument of authority. If self-improvement were a true goal of administration, administrators would universally institute a system of faculty questionnaires that would evaluate the administrators' performance and would be the basis of their salaries and continued employment. This will not happen. Administrators, however, should not be taken too seriously. Individuals do not remain in one administrative position very long before, in corporate fashion, they are promoted or demoted. The average stay of a university president in any institution is only a few years. Despite this fact, elaborate inauguration ceremonies are held for each new president. As the poet Carl Sandburg said regarding politicians: "Now you see 'em, now you don't." In administration, like politics, nothing accumulates.

In another direction within the modern university is the colossus governing student activity, those offices and professions that draw the student away from studies to acquire "life experiences" and perform volunteer work. Such professionals cater to student needs or perceived needs with offices of every kind for every emergency and facilities that go far beyond the requirements of an average social life. This world of student management has its own organizations and publications, its own rarified mentality. Indeed, the sun never sets on administration or student activities management. It is a living for many, able constantly to take the shape of the times.

All this is a kind of authority with which pedagogical authority must contend. It is a world of resistance and inertia, surrounding the living organism of teaching and learning that has its allegiance only to the subject matter, to wisdom, a knowledge of things divine and human. The teacher and the student who perceive the reality of the community of scholars and wish to pursue its great conversation must always cope with these agencies of intrusion. To do so they must don a mask. They must practice the age-old art of the scholar: partial visibility. To gloss a line in Lawrence Ferlinghetti's *Pictures of the Gone World*, the world of teaching and learning is a beautiful place to be born into, but then right in the middle of it comes the professional administrator.

Administration and its associated student agencies and programs are the polis in modern terms that threatens the life of the mind, for the management of the life of the mind is never the life of the mind. The management mind does not inquire. It organizes what it does not understand very well and uses the rest of its energy to promote its own reality. It would make everything its own size.

You may ask if what I say is true. It is a strange tale. It might be otherwise. In fact, looking back on it, it is too sordid to be true. Only Machiavelli would see things in this way. It is something that only Franz Kafka or Eugène Ionesco would describe, and you may wish to disregard it. It is perhaps only the truth of an illusion, too disturbing to consider. You have asked me for my views on the claims of instruction, and I have been diverted into topics not my own that are best left unsaid. Allow me to return to the question of pedagogical authority in teaching and learning.

My final thought concerns the truth of the Socratic model: Socratic ignorance, Socratic method, and Socratic irony. I gave my views in my earlier letter concerning eloquence in relation to the lecture and the general speech of the teacher. What of the process of discussion? For this too is an essential part of the pedagogical process. A good course of instruction will involve periods both of lecture and of discussion, as well as conversation with individual students, outside of class. Socrates is known for his questioning, but he lectures much in Plato's *Dialogues*.

Ernst Cassirer ends the fourth volume of his *Philosophy of Symbolic Forms* with a discourse on Socrates. He says: "As soon as we believe that we have grasped the 'true' face of Socrates and of Socratic thought, then this 'truth' dissolves. Our 'knowledge' is transformed into 'ignorance.' Socrates seems to defy every attempt to 'pin him down'; his every aspect immediately turns into its opposite. This is a fundamental part of Socratic irony. This 'irony' has been borne out again and again in the historical interpretations of the figure of Socrates." Cassirer asks: "Is Socrates a theoretician or a practician? Is he most concerned with a problem of knowledge or is he only concerned with practical action?"

This dialectic between the theoretical and practical is

what motivates the discussion of the truth of a text or subject matter in humane thought. Socrates is the inventor of the question. The question opens up the subject. The starting points of thought are always metaphors. Thus in studying a text the student should first be directed to locate the metaphors, the "root metaphors," so to speak. The meaning of these metaphors becomes the subject of the question. What is held in the metaphor begins to be cognizable. One question always leads to another because we are always ignorant of the shape of the whole.

To see what I mean concerning the interplay of metaphor and question, consider Descartes, who, although he dismisses rhetoric and poetic from his method of truth, is a master of metaphor. The theme of light dominates his work. He transforms this theme into his doctrine of *clarté*, used as the test for an indubitable assertion. Light is the medium of divine knowledge, the opposite of which is his dark image of an anti-God or evil genius, the *malin génie* that can induce ultimate doubt in the knower. There is the Promethean image of Descartes seated in his stove-heated room, the *poêle*, forging the new method that will guide right reasoning. Then there are Descartes's questions. How can the question of my own existence be illuminated by reason such that I can be certain that I am? Can I then also be certain of God's existence and of the world around me? The French feminist philosopher Michèle Le Doeuff, in her book *The Philosophical Imaginary*, has shown how all philosophies depend upon leading metaphors. Descartes is an easy example.

Descartes is also a master of irony. In the dedicatory letter to his *Meditations*, addressed to the faculty of theology at the Sorbonne, Descartes says that he has always thought that God and the soul are the two most important topics to command philosophical attention and are to be proved with the aid of philosophy instead of theology. He says: "It is of course quite true that we must believe in the existence of God because it is a doctrine of Holy Scripture, and conversely, that we must believe Holy Scripture because it comes from God."

To move from his first claim concerning philosophical proof to this statement is an act of ironic genius. To say that God exists because it says so in Holy Scripture and that Holy Scripture is true because it is the word of God is the classic example of a most elementary fallacy in logic—that of *petitio principii*, begging the question or arguing in a circle. What is to be proved is already assumed. Theology is nothing more than the elaboration of this circle. The theologians whom Descartes is addressing believe the medieval claim that philosophy is the servant of theology. Descartes will free philosophy from this servitude. Given the power of the theologians at Paris in his day, one wonders how Descartes got away with this grand joke.

The trope of the poet is metaphor, but the trope of the philosopher is irony. Irony like metaphor never states something literally. What is literally said always diverts our attention to something that cannot be literally said. With our ingenuity we can see something that cannot be put completely into words. The great works of the canon are always typified by the interplay of the elements of metaphor, the question (present either explicitly or implicitly), and irony. These elements in turn must guide discussion of the works of the canon. The dialectic that will always govern discussion between teacher and student is that between the theoretical significance of the works and their practical import. Socrates, the lover of wisdom, is the model of the humanist. Can the great conversation that is teaching ever settle for anything less?

You have asked for my views and I have freely given them. There is an old principle that to say what something is one must say what it is and what it is not. I have tried to do this in an exercise of academic freedom. I hope that you may receive my views in this letter as kindly as you did those of the previous one. But should these letters fall into the hands of people unfamiliar with my ways of thinking, I ask that they know my attachment to the work of the great jurisconsult Hugo Grotius, who was called by the king of France the "miracle of Holland." Grotius said of his work on law that "if anything has here been said by me inconsistent with piety, with good morals, . . . or with any aspect of the truth, let it be as if unsaid." I hold my sentiments with Grotius, and I await your reply.

3 ON THE PEDAGOGY OF IDEAS

You have allowed some time to pass before replying to my last letter, and your good humor has persisted. You express appreciation for my projections on eloquence and authority, for which I am grateful. Your initial request allowed me to speak my mind on those subjects, but now you wish me to go further, to define the medium and purpose of humane education. In this letter I address the nature of ideas as the medium of education. In another letter, if your interest remains, I will speak of the purpose of education, which I see as tied to the idea of a canon.

I believe you are correct when you say that the purpose of science is to discover the nature of things. What metaphysics has claimed to do in thought, science does in fact.

Science says, with Francis Bacon, that nature is to be obeyed in order to be commanded. In science, desire takes two forms, the desire to know what is there before us and the desire to command it, to apply our ingenuity to it. No sooner is one form of this desire partially satisfied than the other takes over. As you say, science is pulled in these two directions. Scientific progress contains a dialectic of these forms, and they are the two senses of science that circulate throughout scientific education.

As a scientist you hold that there is nothing wrong with the application of scientific discoveries to life. In fact it is essential and of great benefit. But, you caution, if application were to become the prime goal of science we would lose science as a search for truth, that is, as the search to understand nature on its own terms. I do not disagree with these views.

Descartes announced that the key to right reasoning in science is method. With the centrality of method comes modernity, with its focus on efficient ordering in all areas of life. Education becomes the quest for certainty in thought and application in practice. Education in this way is hands-on activity and the preparation for hands-on activity. The ivory tower as a place of withdrawal, of intellectual meditation, the pursuit of truth, cultivation of the passions, and freedom of speech is an anti-ideal. In our time it has been deconstructed into centers for research. No one today speaks, except derisively, of the ivory tower. The *tour d'ivoire* is lost, a thing of yesterday, as much forgotten as the nineteenth-century French poet and critic who coined the phrase, C. A. Sainte-Beuve. The ivory tower was never a positive image, but it held a truth—that the university was a relief from the world, a tradition established when Plato acquired a tract of land dedicated to Hecademus and founded his school there, on the outskirts of Athens. The ivory tower in a pure form never existed. Throughout his life Plato connected philosophy and politics, making his trips to Syracuse to the court of the tyrant Dionysius and his opponent, Dion.

Plato's school established the means of Western education, and from this means we can establish the purpose, at least, of humanistic as well as scientific education. This purpose of a community of scholars is presupposed in the *studia generalia* of the earliest medieval universities at Bologna and Paris and later at Oxford, and is continued in the Renaissance conception of the *studia humanitatis*, although each program differs significantly from the other.

Plato invented the pedagogy of ideas. He took this from Socrates. In my previous letter I wrote that I believe Socrates to be the inventor and master of the question. When something can become an idea it can become a problem: a question can be generated with the idea as its guide and motivation. Ideas can be questioned. The idea is both a topos for thought and a standard for criticism. The concern with ideas, as it is brought through the Middle Ages to Locke, and into our time, is the basis of both scientific and humanistic thought. Education is about ideas. Humane education is about how ideas relate to the self, as opposed to how ideas relate to what is other than the self. Ideas are the medium through which the self is in dialogue with itself. In science, ideas are the medium of understanding of what is not part of this inner speech.

The humanities proper (philosophy, history, and literature) and the sciences proper (physical, behavioral, and social) have different interests, as I mentioned earlier, and there is no reason to attempt to synthesize them. Each individual lives with this split in the world every day: the awareness of the extent to which everything in experience relates to the individual and the extent to which everything is something on its own. The individual is not an entity closed within itself; its reality, as William James says in *The Principles of Psychology*, extends to the clothes, dwelling, and possessions of the individual. The demonstration of this, as James points out, is the fact that we may more quickly and deeply offend someone by criticism of that person's clothes, house, or possessions than of his or her opinions or person. We live within the distinction between the inner self of the humanists and the outer world of the sciences. Life is always doubling up. Education follows this doubleness, and there is no reason it should not. True education involves both the humanistic and the scientific approaches to experience.

Ideas constitute a world. An idea can never be contemplated as alone. Ideas make sense only in relation to other ideas. That is why we speak of ideas as something to be discussed. In this way, ideas follow Wilhelm von

Humboldt's conception of a language as having an "inner form." Each language is a world, a total set of meanings that depend upon each other. Ideas are reachable and discussable only within such worlds, but the world of ideas lies beyond any given linguistic world. The same idea can be discussed within each language and requires the symbolism and structures of a particular language to approach its meaning. Education in more than one language allows us to approach ideas differently.

Ideas are the stock-in-trade of the educator. To entertain ideas is the mark of the educated person. Everyone has ideas, in a sense, but to know what great ideas are and to be able to speak about them is the essence of having an education. Great ideas are full-blooded, to recall Longinus's term mentioned in my earlier letter on eloquence. Full-blooded ideas are capable of expansion when brought into contact with an interpreter. The process of interpretation can bring out the dimension of an idea and connect it to other ideas and contexts. In this sense there is a world of ideas and a theater of ideas in which this world is realized.

This theater of ideas is the play of the mind, the mind's ability to release itself to the activity of ideas and to become absorbed in the roles ideas can play in the process of interpretation. The educated mind learns to engage in this play and to gain from it. When education becomes a quest for certainty and practice, the play of ideas is eliminated or reduced to the phenomenon of "brainstorming," in which ideas become instruments to be put to work in the accomplishment of tasks. They also become commodities to be traded from one problem-solving situation to another. An idea successfully put to work in one area may be useful in another. In this process a search for good ideas is the fulfillment of specific aims, but there is no search for the Good, the ultimate idea that can inform human moral practice.

You have asked me what the humanist wishes to accomplish. What is the sense of ideas that the humanist wishes to inject into the process of education? To answer this requires a short digression. You may recall that *idea* is cognate with the term canonized by Plato, *eidos*. The first meaning of *eidos*, and one that is to be found in Homer, is "what one sees," "appearance," "shape," normally of the body. The pre-Socratics use it in this sense. *Idea* is from *idein*, "to see," thus similar to *eidos*. By the time of Herodotus, both *eidos* and *idea* had come into use, and a more abstract meaning had been attached to them, as "characteristic property" or "type."

The *eide* became the basis of Plato's metaphysics. They first appear as a hypothesis in the *Phaedo* (100B–101D), but nowhere in his *Dialogues* does Plato give a proof for their existence. The *eide* are a supersensible reality that we know in various ways by *dialektike* and, in a famous scene in the *Meno*, by a process of questioning that provokes recollections (*anamnesis*), in which the individual soul recalls the *eide* it was connected to before its birth. The problems of the status of the *eide* in Plato's metaphysics are well known; sometimes they are spoken of as the cause of sensible phenomena (*aistheta*), and these phenomena are also said to participate (*methexis*) in the *eide.* There is the analogy that as the *aistheta* are combined in the *kosmos*, so the *eide* exist in an "intelligible place" (*topos noetos*) beyond the heavens. Nothing Plato has said about his doctrine of ideas has satisfied subsequent commentary. That in some sense there are ideas has not been given up by philosophy in the course of its history.

In modern empiricism, in Lockean philosophy, an idea is an immediate object or composed of immediate objects of sensation or reflection. For George Berkeley it is an impression of sense or imagination and for David Hume a representation of memory and association as opposed to a direct sense impression. In modern idealism Kant treats an idea as a transcendent concept of reason, a *noumenon*. Hegel presents ideas as the final achievement of reason, culminating in the Absolute Idea of the final chapter of his *Science of Logic*. For Hegel, ideas are the very forms of nature and spirit (*Geist*) as we experience them. Cassirer connects *eidos* with the symbol in his conception of "symbolic form." We live in a world of symbols. Cassirer defines man as the *animal symbolicum*. The symbol is both physical and spiritual. A symbol is a specific physical thing, a breath of wind, a mark on a surface, but at the same time it carries a meaning. Ideas are embodied in symbols and inseparable from them.

To return from this digression, I hold that ideas let us see with the mind's eye what is invisible to the body's eye. The body's eye makes visible what is before it, but this is at the same time something thought. To see the world in terms of ideas is to grasp its intellectual shape. Education requires us to direct vision from the visible to the invisible. Vision stands for the sensible in this case, so we can say that the process of education is to move from the sensible to sense, to find sense in the sensible. The world of ideas, for the humanist, is never completely separate from the visible because ideas are only reached and spoken about through symbols, and the symbol always has a phenomenal presence that resides in the senses, the imagination, or the memory.

Ideas are joined to symbols in the way the mind is joined to the body. The mind, however, always suggests in its power that it could attain a reality apart from the body. The mind sees itself as something in and of itself. The mind is the dominant term in the opposition of mind and body. As in any opposition the terms are not equal; one of them has greater weight at any given moment in their dialectical movement. The mind can never fully grasp the reality of ideas, although it naturally aspires to do so. The idea itself is something beyond its symbolic embodiments. To enter this sense of ideas as ultimate, the mind must be educated by the idea as it is present in the symbol. The enjoyment of ideas begins in the enjoyment of symbols. The power of the symbol originally takes the mind beyond the immediacy of perception, and the symbol as a medium of contemplation frees thought from what is literal and mundane.

In the pedagogical situation, the teacher is in the world of ideas. The student, at least at the beginning, is only barely in this world. It is a rite of passage to read a work of literature or see a work of art and to pass from what it says or the way it looks into what it means. There is likely a similar rite of passage in science, perhaps occurring at the moment when one sees how a scientific explanation really explains, or how a mathematical proof really proves and is not just an exercise to be done. This rite of passage, of which the teacher is the guide, can be arranged in steps; questions can be asked. In literature the work can be talked about in various ways, but finally, to enter into the other side requires what Joyce calls an epiphany, or what Henri Bergson terms an intuition.

In the *Introduction to Metaphysics*, Bergson speaks of the difference between following the actions of a character in a novel, adding up all the traits of the character to determine who the character is, and the sudden insight into the nature of the character, the grasp of the particular reality from which these traits derive. The reader has then reached or begun to reach the plane of the author, the topic from which the author has made the character. This process of epiphany or intuition is required to get to the idea, what the work is about. The teacher in humane education has the task of producing the world of ideas in the student. This is a process of interpretation. The work must be penetrated. There is no clear way to accomplish this. The teacher has little choice but to keep talking, with the aim of producing the insight necessary for ideas in the student.

How can ideas be expressed? Cassirer describes three functions of consciousness: expression, representation, and signification. They correspond to three kinds of symbolism: images, words, and numbers. The linguistic image is tied to the various tropes, especially metaphor. As Vico says, every metaphor is a fable in brief. Expression presents an idea so it can be felt. The metaphor, like the story, allows us to feel or enter into the subject and presents a meaning, an idea, as if we could see it. The metaphor affects our imagination and enables us to retain in our memory what is said.

The power of words as emphasized in ordinary mental language is to represent the world to us discursively. The *discursus* of ordinary speech allows us to inventory the world, to run through its contents and grasp things in a classificatory manner. The things of experience can be named and brought under classes and orders of classes. This is language in its empirical and commonsensical use. It allows us to grasp an idea in terms of its connection to our practical ability and in terms of our common logical understanding.

To these two modes of symbolism, number adds the sense of technical formulation or technical speech. A dictionary of any natural language shows language to be a system or a circle, in that all words are used to define each other. Any natural language has a grammar that determines the order of words to achieve meaning. Number presents the ideal of unambiguous formulation, in which each element in a system stands in definite and explicit relations to all other elements. This sense of symbolism indicates that any idea can be spoken of in a purely technical way, in a language that aims at mathematical precision. Such a language is a technical vocabulary that can be composed of terms that do not explicitly use mathematical symbolism but embody the sense of system that number represents.

These three functions of consciousness overlap and indicate the ways in which ideas can be approached. The teacher quite naturally employs all of them, but their deliberate use may improve the interpretation of the text for the student. The three modes of symbolism can be employed in instruction in two ways: the teacher, in speaking, may go back and forth among them in the attempt to convey an idea, and a text can be read in terms of finding these three modes in it.

You have asked me to supply examples. Alfred North Whitehead, in the final part of *Process and Reality*, faces the problem of presenting to the reader the idea of God that is in his cosmology. He states this in the technical terms of his philosophy, giving a precise "numerical" formulation of God as an "actual entity" that has a "consequent" and a "primordial" nature. Thus we learn how God is understood as connected to the other entities of Whitehead's system. Surrounding these technical statements are common-sense statements about God's nature that are part of our ordinary understanding of God as an object of religion, as an ultimate term of our experience.

Whitehead also expresses what he means in a metaphor. The problem with which he is struggling is God's relation to the world, which remains problematic in his philosophy. Whitehead suddenly says: "God is the great companion—the fellow-sufferer who understands." This image enters the reader's memory and combines with the other two modes of statement to bring us into Whitehead's meaning. If Whitehead is successful, the reader now sees something of Whitehead's idea of God that is like Bergson's passing from the list of traits of a character into the nature of the character.

A similar approach might be to Dylan Thomas's poem, *Fern Hill.* The poem is fully metaphorical; in every line, metaphors are put upon metaphors. The reader is made to feel the sense in which the child lives in a world without time, in which time and the movement it entails toward death has no effect. "Time let me play and be / Golden in the mercy of his means." At the end of the poem, time has caught up with childhood, or it will catch up with it. The poem ends: "Time held me green and dying / Though I sang in my chains like the sea." To comprehend the poem we not only enter into its metaphors, we also must realize that behind them are the common-sense divisions we make in the world that can be spoken of discursively—time, death, nature, childhood.

The world represented to us through the discursive power of language that is presumed in the poem is the background on which the poem plays. We can see where these ordinary distinctions come into the poem and form its basis. Further, the poem could be spoken of in the technical terms and devices developed to analyze poetry—to look at its structure and meter. All of this allows us to grasp more than what is visible on the surface of the poem and lets it enter into the mind's eye of our thought.

This threefold presentation of ideas is also applicable to works of history when they are read as part of the world of letters and not of social scientific research. History in this humanistic sense is an art of memory that engages in palingenesis, in bringing the past back to life in language. History as a humanity is a narrative that depends on the devices of fiction, but unlike fiction it is grounded in and returns to empirical fact. We encounter this sense of narrative in both the ancients and the moderns, in Thucydides and Tacitus as well as Guicciardini and Gibbon, Michelet and Toynbee. History as narrative naturally invokes both metaphor and discursive thought. But to what extent is it "numerical"? The significative function of consciousness seeks a conceptual order that can be stated in technical terms. History is more than story, more even than a story that is true to fact. For both history and science, a fact is a fact only in relation to a theory.

Ideas can be captured for the student in three ways. I would call it the threefold method of ideas. An idea can be captured in a metaphor that stimulates the student's imagination, in ordinary statements that relate to the student's common-sense experience, and in terms that appeal to the student's desire for technical, structural understanding. The humanist teacher, speaking about philosophy, literature, and the arts, or history and related topics, must employ all three ways of grasping ideas. They are rooted in the functions of consciousness through which we have any kind of knowledge. They are focal points which the teacher may hold in mind when attempting to convey a basic idea. The humanist deals in great ideas as we encounter them in the works of great minds.

In emphasizing the role of ideas in humanistic education I do not mean to ignore the forms in which these ideas are conveyed—myths, fables, stories, maxims, dialogues, and essays. Ideas, in their connections with other ideas, require a medium of expression. The texts of the humanist take many forms. It is beyond my purpose here to describe how each might be approached, lest I offer you not a letter but a treatise, but particularly central to humanistic thought is the narrative. Any idea has an intellectual story surrounding it. The narrative sense of things is not difficult to see in history or literature. It is generally at the basis of these fields, no matter how narrative is to be understood.

Philosophy is also narrative. It is common to think of philosophy as being about arguments: philosophers are thought to produce arguments, and the task of interpreting established philosophies is regarded as searching out the arguments they contain and evaluating them. But arguments, like ideas, do not stand alone. Arguments always require a larger context in which to make sense. This larger context may be explicit or only presupposed. Great philosophies are speeches in which arguments occur as moments. This is true whether they are about what the ancients would call *to ontos on*, the really real, or whether they are about more limited aspects of the real, human knowledge or human conduct. Minute philosophies are little speeches, but speeches nonetheless. Such speeches narrate their subject, that is, they put together the elements of their subject in a coherent fashion. Vico says that doctrines must take their beginnings from the subject matter that they treat. Great philosophies, like great histories or literary works, give us a sense of beginning, middle, and end.

I would also remark on something frequently overlooked in today's instruction in the humanities. This is what we might, following Vico, call the "philologico-philosophical" method. This method prevents us from speaking out of context. Books are always about other books; words are always about other words. Each word has a memory. Words do not mean what they say. Each has an etymology and a meaning that it commands at a particular time in a particular work. To put this philosophically, questions of meaning precede questions of truth. To raise critical questions about a work as though we know what its important words mean is mistaken. Once this critical process is begun it is very difficult to return to questions of meaning. If I were to say to a child, "Would you go into the yard and see if there are any hedychiums there?" the reply would be, "What are hedychiums?" It is as simple as that. Questions of meaning precede questions of truth.

The *ars critica* is useless unless it is preceded by philological understanding—by understanding what is meant, at the time of the work to be interpreted, by a word, an image, a deed, a custom, a law. Only then can we proceed to an evaluation of the work, a consideration of its truth. Students are prone to take words or things referred to in a classic text to mean whatever they take them to mean in their world today. They come to the text as critics. Criticism is rapidly defused and rightly delayed by posing questions of meaning, which must be answered carefully.

This is not a special problem for the sciences, which, by nature of their purpose, do not play upon the ambiguity of words. Scientific textbooks present their materials in contemporary language coupled with stipulative and precising definitions of the basic terms. The language of science strives to present its meanings straightaway. It does not approach language as a theater of memory, full of dialectical tension and ambiguities. Science aims at clarity and directness of language and thought, and this is as it should be.

Whitehead speaks, in *The Function of Reason*, of the reason of Odysseus and the reason of Plato. Odysseus puts reason to work to solve the problem at hand, and by solving a series of problems he arrives home to Ithaca, his goal. Ideas are of interest for him only to the extent they may have some foreseeable consequences. Odysseus is clever; he has the reason of the fox. Plato's reason is that of speculation. Plato shares reason with the gods. Ideas transport their pursuers to what is invisible in the world. This is the aim of speculation. Speculation allows us to see into things. It leads us away from ordinary activity, and, as both Plato and Aristotle are famous for saying, it requires leisure.

It is the leisure that is gone from the modern university, from modern teaching and learning in the humanities and in the sciences. It is not even the reason of Odysseus that we follow today, because Odysseus is on a journey that is governed by his vision of home, his return to himself and his right place. We are left with the reason of the fox, the eternal instrumentalist. The modern corporate university puts everyone to work on the matter-at-hand. It is Hegel's curious scene, that he calls, in an almost untranslatable phrase, *das geistige Tierreich und der Betrug oder die Sache selbst*: the "mental zoo," "humbug," or the "thing-to-be-done," in which all are busy at their own research, each unit a cage beside another cage, held together by university management, high humbug, a flurry of activity, reports, committees, new proposals, "self-studies," and growth-assessment.

I will not go on, lest I say too much. You may not agree with all I have said. You will, I think, agree with much of what I have said about ideas and their nature, but who would agree with my pessimism about their current status? Optimism and pragmatism are the watchwords of the day, and they are qualities that are expected of academics and of the public at large. There is no pessimistic science.

THE PEDAGOGY
OF THE AGES

I AM glad to have your general agreement regarding my views that ideas are the medium of humanistic education, even though, as I suspected, you do not share my pessimism about the current state of things. I agree that ideas are also the basis of scientific education, but, as you say, they are dealt with in a different way. In scientific work, ideas are not guides to life, to values and conduct. They serve as guides for empirical, theoretical, and experimental activity. But both of these dimensions of ideas are testament to the importance of ideas.

For the humanist, ideas are not only objects to be grasped in themselves; they appear in history. The humanist mentality is narrative in form and involves the

concept of ages. This is essentially the idea of a ca
standard that has arisen in time and has gained
thority that time confers on anything, what is com
called tradition. The sciences operate primarily w
canon of the present, the humanities with a canon o
past. I mentioned this idea of a canon in my last le
and said something of its importance in my second let
You now ask to know more precisely what I mean, and
am happy to respond. You provide me with an opportu
nity to think through this rather unpopular idea.

As you have pointed out, past research is continually
surpassed by present research. I have been told that scientific journals have a life of perhaps ten years. Research
that is more than a decade old or so can generally be dis-
missed. It is of interest primarily to the historian of science, or in rare cases to the working scientist for some
point that might accidentally survive. Science is progressive. Beyond the immediate past, which is the beginning
point of new research, truly past scientific discoveries are
obsolete.

For the humanist conception of knowledge and education it is the reverse. Everything depends upon the past,
upon the history of words, customs, laws, values, and
aesthetic images. The humanist has but one school,
which has been called the *School of Ages* by Harold
Bloom. The scientist relies upon what I would call the
School of the Present. This is as it should be, for there are
things to be known by the disregard for what has gone
before and other things to be learned by immersion in the
forest of history—the *sylva sylvarum* of memory.

As you say, the scientist works against the immediate past. The contemporary physicist works toward new knowledge, against the state of physics today, toward what it can become. Physics today is the result of the whole development of physics from the ancients forward. But it is the result that counts. There is no need to consult Aristotle's *Physics* to make an advance in contemporary physics. This is why Kant in the *Third Critique* (sec. 47) calls Isaac Newton a "big head" rather than a genius, reserving genius for figures in literature and the arts who must remake the entire sense of human aesthetics with each creation. Science is progressive, and even as great a figure as Newton builds from what has been established to something further, in Newton's case, a great deal further. Science works not only within the immediate past to the present, it always looks to the future, and the public is always looking with it, expecting future wonders and new certainties. This is a problem science always faces, as a search for truth itself—the demand to justify itself by applying its results.

The humanist looks to the past. The present is only a place to stand, and the future can be prepared for only by a whole grasp of the past. The humanist takes the Italian poet Giuseppe Ungaretti's statement, "Tutto, tutto, tutto è memoria" ("Everything, everything, everything is memory") as a motto. And further, the humanist accepts the maxim in the *Ricordi* of the Florentine historian Francesco Guicciardini, "All that which has been in the past and is at present will be again in the future. But both the names and the faces of things change, so that he who does not have a good eye will not recognize them. Nor will he know how to grasp a norm of conduct or make a judgment by means of observation." The human "good eye," the *buon occhio*, is the sight of the cycle. The repetitions of the past illuminate. Everything lives out a life in the past and can be impressed on memory. What is not remembered is lost, on occasion remembered and often forgotten yet again.

James Joyce says, "Memory is imagination," following a line in Vico's *New Science*: "La memoria è la stessa che la fantasia" (par. 819), an idea that goes back to Aristotle's seldom read little treatise *On Memory* (450a, 21–23). All the images upon which the artist and humanist thinker can draw are in memory and were at one time in perception. The humanist, as I mentioned above, learns that all books are about other books and that all works of art are about other works of art. Jorge Luis Borges, reflecting on his own work in *This Craft of Verse*, says that, when he thinks of the word "night," he recalls Joyce's line in *Finnegans Wake*: "the rivering waters of, hitherandthithering waters of. Night!" (p. 216). "We feel," Borges says, "that such a line could have been written only after centuries of literature."

One of the talents of the art historian Aby Warburg was his ability in a long lecture to take a contemporary work of art and move it back through older works of art and images to its earliest origins. To see with the good eye is to find the pattern of repetition and alteration of the forms that lie behind the present, whether in the study of art or the study of human conduct. It makes no difference whether the artist deliberately intended to play upon the past or intended to be wholly novel, the past is always there. What it means for the poet to call upon the Muses for a beginning is to hope for an image to appear that is lying dormant in human memory. Another way to put this is Claude Lévi-Strauss's principle that we do not make ourselves through myths; myths make themselves through us.

The Western canon is lost as a guiding principle of humanistic education. It was alive as late as the mid-twentieth century but is now gone with the wind, the disappearance of an old order. In its place are two agencies: one has been called by Bloom the *School of Resentment*; the other is a particular embodiment of it that I would call the *Program of Multiculturalism*. The School of Resentment regards all disagreement over values to be a manifestation of some form of class struggle. All the great narratives are seen to depend upon one or another kind of class interest, which can be understood in economic, political, racial, or gender terms. What appeared to old-fashioned readers as works whose authors reached beyond time to grasp values and the human condition are seen as documents of economic, political, racial, or sexist bias.

This approach coincides with what has been called the "hermeneutics of suspicion." The instrument of this approach is criticism. The "critical eye," as opposed to the "good eye," sees through everything in its own terms. It does not study appearances to discover an underlying principle. It sees through appearances, to reveal the hidden motivations. All becomes ideology. The cultural critic seeming to have an independent Archimedean point has, in fact, an ideology which sees all else as ideology. This approach to culture and thought is not an *ars critica* driven by doubt. Doubt is not suspicion, because doubt can be answered. But what answers suspicion? Nothing can answer suspicion. Critical reflection can be turned back upon itself, and the mind can become suspicious of its own conclusions undertaken originally by suspicion. Suspicion contains no internal principle of its own completion. It is a short step from this to the doctrine of deconstruction.

The mind of deconstruction is what Hegel describes in his *Phenomenology of Spirit* as the stage of the "inverted world." In this stage, consciousness reaches a point, in its attempts to see through appearances, where the world can just as well be the precise opposite of itself. The North Pole may in fact be the South Pole, criminals may in fact be saints, and the reverse. There is no principle that consciousness can forge, having reached this point of its analysis, whether what appears to be real is the way things are or whether the way things are is exactly opposite. Consciousness goes into a swoon. Deconstruction is the content of that swoon, for through its approach a text is seen to be just as much not what it seems to mean as what it seems to mean.

As a literary doctrine, "deconstruction," as coined by Jacques Derrida, refers to a range of critical techniques that reveal logical and rhetorical incompatibilities between the explicit and implicit planes of discourse in a text. It is an especially French logic, which is to think in dyads—to take one side of an opposition that is largely accepted and affirm that if we look harder we will see that exactly the opposite is the case. Thus for Derrida traditional metaphysics, which was thought to be a search for speculative truth, is just a form of white mythology, a kind of lie. For Michel Foucault the view that works had authors with interests and purposes is reversed, and it is asserted that there are in fact no authors. Works are just texts. This is the inverted world Hegel describes, because it claims that, if we thought metaphysics was a search for truth, or that books had authors, we might just as well hold the opposite. All might be one way as well as the other. There is only the commitment to showing the opposite, not to holding it as a truth. From our original suspicion that has led us to the abandonment of metaphysics or the author, we commence further to take things apart.

All is deconstructable, including deconstruction. What is to stop us? The outcome of Hegel's inverted world is the sudden realization by consciousness of the existence of the ego. Whatever the interpretation of appearance, consciousness realizes that it is a process happening to it as an "I," an ego. Inversion is not only a swoon of the ego, it is also a self-indulgence of it. Resentment is a form of self-indulgence, and it can keep the intellectual ego busy for a long time. There seems no end to textual studies and cultural studies.

The Program of Multiculturalism enters the School of Resentment at this point, because it sees the Western canon as elitist. Cultures are anything one wants them to be. Whatever one chooses that is new or nontraditional, or to one's particular liking, is as valuable as anything in the canon. The lyrics of Bob Dylan are of as much merit as those of Dylan Thomas. The thoughts of Jim Croce are as valuable as those of Benedetto Croce. Who is to say? Only the ego, as it goes about its business without the standard or baggage of the past. The canon is a kind of memory system that allows us to approach anything new and to connect it to what was. The works of the canon are distinguished by the fact that they can be read over and over. They contain images and ideas that can never be exhausted because they put us in touch with the nature of the human self.

The test for whether a work is acceptable to the School of Resentment and its Program of Multiculturalism is whether it aims at cultural change. Such works have a sense of exposé. The reader is surprised and fascinated by what is revealed. Works that deliberately embody the ideologies of resentment or that are so regarded by its supporters should not be read more than once. If they are read again they become thin and hollow and lose their initial power for social effect. It is like reading a magazine article a second time or trying to teach it in a class. There is little else to be learned than what seemed so vital and attractive the first time.

In *The Western Canon* Bloom presents his own list of works for the Western canon, divided into ages based upon Vico and Joyce—the Theocratic Age, including works of ancient Greek and Latin literature, some Sanskrit and ancient Chinese works, the Koran, and a few examples of medieval literature; the Aristocratic Age, a span of five hundred years from Dante's *Divine Comedy* through Goethe's *Faust, Part Two*; the Democratic Age of the post-Goethean nineteenth century, in which arises Romanticism and Russian and American literature; and the Chaotic Age of contemporary literature for all European countries, Latin America, Africa, Australia, Canada, the United States, and such literary traditions as Yiddish and Hebrew.

These ages are modeled on Vico's ages of gods, heroes, and humans, from his conception of the cycles of history in his *New Science*, with the addition of a fourth age, which Bloom has taken from Joyce's *Finnegans Wake*. Joyce plays on Vico's three ages, adding a fourth in what he calls "our wholemole mill-wheeling vicociclometer" (p. 614). He variously refers to this fourth age in the last term of a series of four words or phrases, such as: "eggburst, eggblend, eggburial, and hatch-as hatch can" (p. 614). Joyce plays on Vico's three principles of human society—religion, marriage, and burial—and adds the fourth state of dissolution. *Finnegans Wake* is itself divided into four parts.

Joyce's divisions differ from the standard ones derived from Hegel's divisions in his *Philosophy of History*. These Hegelian divisions are reflected in a list of "100 Significant Books" found in *Good Reading*, a work prepared by the Committee on College Reading of the College English Association, originally published in 1935 and reprinted and revised many times. You may also have come across this work. My edition is the sixteenth printing of the Mentor paperback of 1960. The list of "100 Significant Books" is divided into ancient, medieval and Renaissance, and each of the centuries of the modern period through the twentieth century. This list focuses strictly on Western works in history, philosophy, and literature, while Bloom's list is primarily works of poetry and fiction, with some sacred texts, and including some works from various non-Western traditions.

Good Reading reflects the sense of a liberal-educated mind of the mid-twentieth century, a mind that has been formed by reading Homer, Aristotle, Plato, and the Bible, Confucius and Virgil, Cellini, Cervantes, Rabelais, and Shakespeare, Descartes, Gibbon, and Donne, Rousseau, Swift, and Voltaire, Austen, Chekhov, Flaubert, Melville, Shelley, and Dreiser, Sandburg, Mann, and Veblen, to mention a sample of the authors on the list of "100 Significant Books." In an introductory essay, "How to Use Good Reading," by Atwood H. Townsend of New York University, we find advice that, although written not that long ago, now appears quaint: "A complete reading program, therefore, should include four factors: at least one good book each week, a newspaper or news magazine, magazines of comment and interpretation, and book reviews. If you keep feeding your intelligence with these four foods, you can be sure your brain cells will not be undernourished. To this must be added the digestive process that comes from your own thinking and from discussion with other people" (p. 15).

It is, I think, an unimaginable program in today's university but one exactly in line with Cicero's conception of the liberal arts, brought up to date. Here is the basis of the great conversation of liberal education that was much spoken of in American education in the 1950s and 1960s and before, in which aspirations at being literate, at expanding one's vocabulary, at being an educated person, were still alive. It is a nostalgic ideal for anyone who experienced it. I expect we share such experience, being of the same generation.

You no doubt recall the debate of the period concerning the separation between what C. P. Snow called the two cultures, the scientific and the literary. This debate appears of no consequence in the face of today's educational cafeteria of subjects and experiences that make up a university education—internships, postcolonial studies, cultural studies, environmental studies, gender studies, queer studies, peace studies, race studies—each of which may have some merit, but within the series there is no center.

The Western canon as such has been lost, despite the fact that there are still significant courses taught in fields of the sciences and the arts, and that there are still students who seek out the classics of ancient and modern thought. The canon has been replaced not by a new canon but by a jumble that looks like a canon. In reality this jumble is a vague ideology of social change to which the student is asked to subscribe. But if the old canon is lost, the *idea* of the canon should not be lost. The sense of the canon as a fixed list of great books is gone. The Chicago Great Books Program, the five-foot shelf of Harvard Classics, or sets of the World's Greatest Literature, are dinosaurs. Is it possible to save the idea of a canon and make it a principle of instruction in the humanities? It is necessary to do so, or instruction in the humanities will become random or simply the instrument of this or that ideological fashion. Fashion is the principle of trivial change. Tradition is the principle of measured change.

You may also recall Ezra Pound's early pamphlet, *How to Read*, in which he writes that each educated person must find an individual canon by looking for books that were turning points, working backward and forward from the origins of literature to contemporary works. Such a canon is idiosyncratic, but not wholly so, for it will in many respects incorporate a sense of the great works of world literature. On this view there is no set list of one-hundred great books, but it presupposes an awareness of an order of books that has emerged in time as those read over and over by the educated.

Within this amorphous collection of world literature one must conduct one's education and find one's own particular canon. This is not simply a list of preferences; it is a canon because it is claimed as a standard that can challenge any conventional order and which may include works that are turning points the conventional order has overlooked. One reads toward the discovery of such an order and, once found, all the rest of literature is opened up. Such a canon is a place from which to read and think, a topos.

The teacher must work to invoke such a process in the student. I think there may be an analogy to this in your concern as a scientist to train the student to be at home in the laboratory. The laboratory is the counterpart of the library. It is the ultimate facility the student needs. To know one's way around a well-equipped laboratory is the hallmark of the scientist, as to know one's way around a good library is the hallmark of the humanist. The aim of liberal education cannot be to establish one list of great books that the student receives externally and learns. The problem of the pedagogy of the ages is to bring students to the point from which it is possible for them to internalize what is read by forming their own canons as a response to the larger and vague list of world literature. The teacher has done this and is thus a living example of what is to be done.

The important thing is the sense of a standard and the sense of forming one's canon against a larger tradition. Without this there is no education. Books are just read, if at all, in various courses, and forgotten. To forge such a canon for oneself requires one to read, to penetrate what various books are in relation to other books, not just to go through books as texts. The aim is to construct a trellis upon which all else can be placed. It begins a lifelong process of revision that is the distinguishing mark of the truly educated. I think we likely agree on this.

Education in this matter is education in discernment. In Pound's later reflections on reading, the *ABC of Reading* (1934), he says that those who hold that "you can't teach literature" are probably correct, but he says: "You *can* quite distinctly teach a man to distinguish between one kind of a book and another." An outcome of this, for example, is Pound's assertion that "mediocre poetry is in the long run the same in all countries." We might add to this Oscar Wilde's observation, that all bad poetry is sincere. The development by the student in such discernment builds confidence that it is possible to make judgments of taste.

Taste is more than what I happen to like. It is a standard pursued, that can take form only in the individual's attempt to command it. Taste is perhaps learned first by imitation and later by claiming it for oneself, but it is the mark of education, and although it may differ from one person to another it is recognized as a standard among educated people. Confronted with one person's canonical judgments of taste, one may create changes in one's own intellectual stance. Taste is what stands for the humanist between personal preference (which is a subject of investigation for behavioral science) and proof (which is a subject for logic and the mathematical sciences). The books that one may absorb at age twenty-five are not the ones that may attract at forty-five or that may affect one at sixty-five and older.

Pound says: "I believe the ideal teacher would approach any masterpiece that he was presenting to his class *almost* as if he had never seen it before" (p. 86). The masterpiece can be reread every year; on each reading it seems as though one has never quite read it before. One's ability to perceive what is there changes with one's interest and age, just as what is in a book for one historical age will differ from what is in it for another. Reading is an activity of self-knowledge, wherein the self confronts itself and builds for itself an intellectual autobiography.

A great work is always a mirror of the soul, and the canon one develops is the trellis of the soul as well as much of its content. The instructor in the humanities must keep this in mind. Reading is our way of enacting the inscription on the temple of Apollo at Delphi—*gnothi seauton*, "know thyself"—and it is also a way of approaching its second maxim—*meden agan*, "nothing too much"—because such reading is the encounter with all the values known to the self. It is in the canon that we find the problem of the best life and the alternatives upon which to act in any situation. In history, philosophy, and literature the human condition is portrayed as fully as it ever can be.

By now you have heard enough, I expect, of these ideals. It will be difficult to find teachers who are dedicated to them among those who have not been educated under them. It may be too late to save the art of reading; it may remain a privilege of the old, those who have been educated to it. Most of education is organized against it; but if it is made available, some may take it up. There has been much consideration in some institutions of a "core" course for undergraduate students. The principle is that, although there is no perfect list of books to read, if some works are read by all then a basis of common thought is established, and perhaps a common basis for intellectual conversation.

You have asked for practical advice in this matter. I will oblige you with two suggestions. One is to put into a single course the aim of the European *Gymnasium*—a study of the origins. This is to read the original documents of the Judeo-Christian and the Greco-Roman traditions: basic parts of the Old Testament, for example, selections from the Hebrew scriptures, the five books of Moses, especially Genesis, and from the books of the "Prophets," also from the "Writings," especially Job, Ecclesiastes, and the Song of Solomon (Judeo-); the New Testament, for example, the Gospels (Matthew, Mark, Luke, John), Acts, Romans, Revelation (-Christian); Homer's *Iliad* and *Odyssey* (Greco-), and selections from the *Digest* of Roman law, especially those parts that establish conceptions of property, marriage, and civic duties (-Roman).

This tetralogy would present the student with all the biblical images and stories, with the range of Greek gods and heroes and the one great work of Roman genius upon which all later law and Western society is founded. What is essentially contained in these first works is that to which all else refers. The student would have a much better access to any later work, whether it be Joyce or Milton, Dante or Shakespeare, Montaigne or Machiavelli, Plato or Augustine. It is a course on first books, that might stand to literature as Aristotle says logic or the *organon* stands to the study of the sciences—a necessary prerequisite.

A second version of a core course might be a range of seven books that are fundamental and pass through the ages. Here is one possibility: the Book of Job (Job is one of the original portraits of man and nature); Homer's *Odyssey* (the Trojan War is the first event of Western secular culture, and because the *Odyssey* would also involve some discussion of the *Iliad*); Plato's accounts of the last days of Socrates (*Euthyphro*, *Apology*, *Crito*, *Phaedo*) (Socrates is the archetypal figure of reason in Western consciousness); Dante's *Inferno* (Dante is the summary of the metaphysical imagination of the Middle Ages); Shakespeare's *Hamlet* or *King Lear* (Shakespeare is the greatest poet of English, the students' own language); Goethe's *Faust* (the Faust myth is a key to modern man); and Freud's *Lectures on Psychoanalysis* (Freud is the founder of our modern view that the contemporary individual has an internal monologue).

I am sure you would agree that there is no one perfect list, but the student could certainly do worse than to read these seven books. They focus on images of the self and thus allow for an immediate engagement of the reader. The student studying in an American university, whether or not that student's background is Western, must understand the Western self first, because no matter who the student is, the student is present in this tradition. From the specific canon the student develops, that student can go anywhere in world literature and comprehend other works that are not part of the original canon, or that constitute parallel canons with dialectical connections to each other. One begins with one's self where one is, then one can go anywhere. The student can study various canons together; they need not go in any sequence. But there is ultimately to be a canon of one's own. It, like a mother tongue, allows one to acquire other languages, but there is always the mother tongue and the heart which it informs.

As you know, I have always been very interested in the literature of other cultures, especially the sacred books of the East, but I have made no attempt to incorporate them in the above. This is because I believe they require their own treatment, as do the myths of other cultures such as those found in Barbara Sproul's collection of *Primal Myths*. I have throughout my career taught a course in Eastern classics, including such works as the *I Ching*, *The Secret of the Golden Flower*, *The Tibetan Book of the Dead*, the *Tao te Ching*, the *Lankâvatâra Sûtra*, and the literature of Zen Buddhism. I also have taught, as part of the philosophy of culture, the works and traditions of many cultures both archaic and contemporary. The canons of these literatures are part of my own, but they are too extensive to relate here, and I have already tried your patience. My grasp of these literatures would not have been possible had I not constructed in my own way the canon of my own culture, which is a lengthy and arduous process.

We might say of this process what Hegel says of the acquisition of philosophy. One cannot substitute a feeling within one's breast that one is educated for the actual process of education, any more than one can claim chicory to be equal to coffee. Because one has opinions it does not follow that one has taste, or because one has a mind that one is educated, any more than because one has a foot one can make shoes.

Now you have heard me out, and I continue to admire your kindly patience, for as I have said before, these are the meditations of a humanist who sees himself in an inhumane world, who would say with Jean-Jacques Rousseau, quoting Ovid in exile on the Black Sea, "Here I am the barbarian because no one understands me" (*Tristia*, 5.10.37). I claim this with the modest hope that you have understood, but if not, that you will at least continue to stand to these views as a friend who has not been made the worse for hearing them.

Postscript: On Technology

HAVING concluded my last letter, I realize that I neglected to respond to the part of your original question concerning the role of technology in education. I can add only a few words on this topic, which will likely raise more problems than they will solve, as I know little on the subject. The medium of technology is information, and the medium of information is the computer. Information is different from ideas or narrative. Information is a commodity that can be traded and consumed. Ideas depend upon thought and involve patience and epiphany. Ideas require internalization, as do narratives. Information is an object to be reflected upon and used instrumentally. The electronic classroom deals in what can be communicated, what can be passed from one person to another and can be rearranged and used to produce an intellectual product. It treats ideas as information and cannot do otherwise because electronic processes are not thought.

Bertrand Russell said of logic, we engage in logic not in order to think, but in order not to think. This is true of the computer. To access everything is to access nothing. Everything and nothing, as Hegel says at the beginning of his *Science of Logic*, are equally indeterminate. Ideas, unlike information, take the self out of itself and produce meanings that are unreachable and that can be achieved only noetically. The teaching of ideas is a slow process that requires the making of a mental life, the formulation of an intellectual personality. The danger of the electronic classroom is that it is virtual knowledge in the way that the electronic battlefield engages in virtual battles. Virtual knowledge is the acquisition of information and its application to problems.

In the complex of e-mail, Internet, and similar systems, the teacher becomes a guide, directing the student's attention to this or that and answering questions, in the way that a park ranger takes one on a nature trail or a docent guides one through a museum. It is an informative, not a spiritual, process. It is not Virgil guiding Dante through the *Inferno* of the *Divine Comedy*. Virgil accompanies Dante as a guardian, in the way that the traditional teacher aims at beginning the process of self-knowledge in the pupil. Information leaves the pupil just where the pupil is, in terms of the human power of thought. Traditional education engages the pupil in culture, in the progressive formation of the human self and the way the life of the self can be transformed by ideas.

Hegel says, in the third part of his *Encyclopedia*, the *Philosophy of Spirit*, that the educated person is known by the possession of memory. Memory is required for learning, and it is in memory we attempt to place a developing and coherent view of the world. This is why Memory is the Mother the Muses, and why the Muses, her daughters, are the arts of humanity. Information requires only the memory of the computer, the sense of a vast warehouse from which items can be stored and ordered up, to be brought to bear on specific problems. Solving specific problems is part of the process of the educated mind, but there is the further problem of the ordering of the soul, grasping the True as the whole, the quest for self-knowledge.

The relation of the "divine and the human" which is knowledge that leads to wisdom is not a matter of information and can in principle never be such. The electronic process of information is never a rethinking of anything because it is not thinking in the first place. The acquisition of an education requires the association with other people who are educated. They cannot be met over the Internet, for education is not a matter of virtual encounters with other minds; it is a matter of actual encounters with the human self in its educated form.

How many times will we be told that these systems are just a tool that can improve education? A moment's reflection will tell us that a tool is always an extension of the self, and what the tool will allow is what we will become as we use it. The electronic classroom will continue and expand. Teachers can and will continue to be on duty twenty-four hours a day through e-mail, in which there is a constant trade of information, questions to be answered, and trivial requests for assistance. Teachers are also linked to each other and to the administration in a nonstop world. There are constant requests for responses.

The computer world is an ongoing wonder, a *Wunderkammer*, but one in which little is truly interesting or amazing. It is a dead-serious world, on which the sun never sets. Foolishness is not allowed and irony is not possible. Technology is a new religion in which everyone is a convert. Never before has humanity taken upon itself, in all countries, at all levels, and through individual initiative, the mastery and use of such a new order of things. Everyone, everywhere, learns, as an act of free will, the use of the computer. Joyce might describe it as something to which "Here Comes Everybody."

Jacques Ellul, whom I mentioned in my first letter, in his classic *The Technological Society* says that the average person is fascinated with performance. In the technological society all is performance. The danger is that all instruction can proceed this way. Time spent in the classroom begins to appear as clumsy as letter writing and postal mail. The class meeting is a coda, an afterthought where things are pulled together, loose ends tied up. The classroom ceases to be a sacred precinct, the precinct of Hecademus, in which the importance of thought and thought itself can appear. It is a variable in a total functional system. A class session becomes just a kind of meeting.

The difficulty arises when this phenomenon of the electronic classroom reaches its second and third generations. Then it transforms instruction into the guiding in information. Those taught according to this in turn teach according to it. What originally seemed an instrument, a new system to aid instruction, becomes instruction itself. It is like the career of the new math, which originally appeared effective only because it presupposed a mathematical mentality developed by the old math. As long as one developed a mathematical mentality, the new math seemed to work. But it proved unable to develop a truly mathematical mentality on its own and required constant modification until something had to be done. The fundamentals had to be rediscovered.

The same process is evident in the abandonment of the old-fashioned use of phonics in language instruction in favor of "finding little words in big words" and spelling words any way one wishes. These new approaches presupposed a spelling mentality to be already present in the student. Then it became apparent that these variations produced students who could not spell, and finally the teachers who were products of the system could not spell either. These reforms of public education have led to the formation of private centers that actually teach students mathematics and spelling.

Do such examples mean that the reduction of education to information or problem-solving will follow the same cycle, and we will arrive back at a sense of the education of the self? We might realize, as programmed learning turns into learning itself, that the education of the self is left out. But it may not follow the course of the above examples; they failed because the product they produced was inferior to the former.

In the case of programmed electronic learning, the product will not fail because it is all-encompassing. It is necessarily self-furthering. The education of the self is not required to make it work. In fact, it is crucial to turn from those humanities that educate the self toward a universal method, toward what is within our reach with the ever-improving tools we have, to turn away from the humane studies, as Descartes advocated in the *Discourse*, when he says that the study of history and fables will only tempt us to become like paladins (tilting at windmills) attempting projects beyond our powers to complete. Whitehead says, in the first two sentences of *The Aims of Education*: "Culture is activity of thought, and receptiveness to beauty and humane feeling. Scraps of information have nothing to do with it." He says further, that "a merely well-informed person is the most useless bore on God's earth." Worse than scraps of information is the world of information, which substitutes for thought and masquerades as the means of education.

Jonathan Swift, I think, saw in advance much of what I have described. Writing at the same time as Vico, Swift is the first, in the "Voyage to Laputa" in *Gulliver's Travels* (1726) and in "A Digression in Praise of Digressions" in *A Tale of a Tub* (1697, 1710), to design and name a computer. *Compotus* (*computus*) goes back to the High

Middle Ages, conceived as a science of exact chronology reckoned by rational means. Swift, the satirist, understood even more possibilities.

In the grand Academy of Lagado, Gulliver is ushered into a large room where a professor and a team of young students are operating a twenty-foot-square engine of knowledge, a contrivance that, with little bodily labor, "may write Books in Philosophy, Poetry, Politicks, Law, Mathematicks and Theology, without the least Assistance from Genius or Study." Swift includes a drawing of this great invention that will give "the World a compleat Body of all Arts and Sciences." In the digression in *A Tale of a Tub* Swift says that "the Method of growing Wise, Learned, and *Sublime*, having become so regular an Affair, and so established in all its Forms," there is no longer anything left to explain such as would fill a whole volume. "This I am told by a very skillful *computer*, who hath given a full Demonstration of it from Rules of *Arithmetick*." Today reality defeats the satirist.

Again, these are remarks likely to offend many. The kinder would wish to inform me of my errors about technology, even if in a high moral tone. Others will find these simply odd ideas, a pursuit of foolishness too misguided to correct. But I appreciate the generosity of your attention to the correspondence, for I know you have other things to do beyond considering these speculations, and I shall not sustain them further.

Index